THIS IS THE KINDNESS

RICHARD PATTERSON III

DEDICATION

This book is dedicated to:

Anyone who has made adjustments in relationships,
To those who feel like their sacrifices have gone unnoticed,
To the mother working over-time to feed her family,
To the father that feels unappreciated,
To the child or young adult that has been neglected and
searching for a sense of identity.

This book is dedicated to those who desire to partner with people for the
purpose of accomplishing goals that benefit others.

My prayer is that this book encourages you not to give up on
yourself or on people

CONTENTS

ACKNOWLEDGEMENTS

Like a fingerprint, the kindness you show expresses your uniqueness.

-Pastor Richard Patterson III

A very special thank you to my mother, Elder Joan Ivory, who is the epitome of kindness. You've taught and still are teaching me what it means to value people. You raised five children all by yourself and somehow still managed to have 'one on ones' with us all. Your energy, drive and work ethic has set the bar high and your class is unmatched. I love you with all of my heart. To the Chief Apostle Eugene Smith Sr. (The Apostle of Love), I honor and love you for being a father to me and for being a consistent presence of sound wisdom and counsel that helps me to make better choices. To my brothers, sisters, aunts, uncles, nieces and nephews, thank you for unconditionally loving and accepting me for who I am. To my church family, Better Covenant, thank you for supporting me, I love you all. To all my friends and colleagues who believe in me and to those who have just prayed for me and interceded on my behalf, thank you. More than anything else, thanks be to God who always causes us to triumph through Christ Jesus. I am thankful for every circumstance that sharpened me and pushed me to get this book out of my spiritual womb. A special thanks to life lessons that brought me to this truth; you are not my enemy, but you are my friend.

RICHARD PATTERSON III

INTRODUCTION

I would like to tell you that I'm a world renowned media mogul or a great entertainer, but I am just a young man who was raised to love God, love people and to be kind no matter what. My desire is to share with you the practical side of your God given greatness. Life has it shares of ups and down, but what we all have in common, as people, is our need for relationship with others. My strongest gift is the ability to discern what another person values in order to partner with them. Through good times and bad times, I learn how to positively assess what kindness means to them. This takes me to what we will discuss in this book, understanding the power of being considerate through listening and identifying what pleases the other person. We all have questions like, 'why are people resistant to my approach? We both share the same need, so let's just get it done.' In this book, I will help you understand that your approach to your relationships may be valid, but your greatness is seen in your ability to identify what serves the needs of others. You may give a lot, but the kindness you show will always reciprocate back to you, even when you're about to give up.

Chapter 1
PARTNERED FOR PURPOSE

Imagine a husband and wife of old age. They are in a dire situation. The wife wants children, but is unable to have any. To make matters worse, they have just received an eviction notice. Unfortunately, they can't stay with relatives, and they must travel far to find a new residence. As they are searching and traveling to find their new place, food becomes scarce. The husband also quickly realizes that he's not the only one that finds his wife beautiful, even in her old age. He knows that in his culture, men of high status will surely kill him and take her to be their wife instead. Have you ever been in a place where you didn't know what to do next? Has life ever brought a situation to your doorstep that made you say, 'I don't have a clue what I should do?'

Well, this husband certainly found himself facing the foe of life. He desperately needed an answer; he needed to know which approach he should take. As they enter the city, he speaks to his wife about his decided solution. He says, "This is the kindness I'm asking you to express towards me when we come into foreign lands." He tells her to say that she is his sister and she consents to lie for her husband. Though this seems foolish and dishonest, our focus is her quick, easy and harmonious agreement. For this wife, being kind to her husband didn't mean cooking a grand, over-the-top meal or spending lavish amounts of money on a gift. The kindness she expressed towards him meant taking the time to hear his heart and then supplying his need. For this book's purpose, the definition of true kindness means hearing and then doing what pleases others.

The story of this husband and wife can be found in the book of Genesis, chapters twelve and twenty. The husband's name is Abraham and his wife is Sarah. When I read this true story years ago, I saw it as a man treating his wife as a piece of property that had no value (which was common in that day). To add insult to injury, I viewed Abraham as a repeat offender, putting Sarah in this same position again some 20 plus years later. His lie causes both monarchical leaders to take further interest in his wife and bring her into their private chambers. In both cases, the leader finds out that Sarah is not Abraham's sister, which causes Abraham to be confronted by them. Luckily for Abraham, they released Sarah and they never took advantage of her.

Initially, my analytical perception of this story caused me to create a negative reality. When it was revealed that Abraham was not lying about Sarah being his sister, (they had the same father, but not the same mother, which was common in that day) this led me to go back to try and understand. As I reread Genesis chapter twenty, I realized that purposeful relationships outlive perception. What we seek to accomplish together determines what kindness means for us. We no longer perceive ourselves as victims, but as partners for purpose. Abraham understood the men of his day were vicious and would kill for beauty. As husband and wife, they talked about what it would take to survive the tough time of famine that they were in. Their conversation went like this, and I paraphrase: "Please baby-baby, please say you're my sister and not my wife. They'll kill me, but because you're so fine, they'll keep you alive. What I mean is, I'm asking you to be the best kept secret and on my behalf, embrace the shame that comes with you making the sacrifice of discretion." We already know that Sarah consents with what he asked. This seemingly irrational and deceptive approach was just an agreement between husband and wife; not a demand. Now let's be honest! Who's signing up for that? Sounds like tomfoolery. Discovering kindness which is the practical side of our God given greatness, can look like foolishness at times, but a wise man said,

"God uses the foolish things of our world to confound the wise."

- Apostle Paul

This story challenged me to rethink my own perception and position on relationship. It's like planning to rent a property for a vacation. You go on the Airbnb website and read the reviews. They seem good, but you talk to a friend who actually rented and stayed at that very property. They tell you that the place was horrible and it looks nothing like the website. Although you were committed and about to book the property, this second opinion sways your decision. Relationships are the same way. You're more likely to have a better experience if you're open to the wise counsel of others.

Accepting wise counsel is easy, but what do you do if you receive foolish words? Approach it as if you are receiving an unnecessary or unwanted gift. Imagine a holiday where someone is extremely excited to give you a gift. You understand the importance of receiving the gift with gladness, so you smile and show no signs of disapproval. Then you have a moment alone. You appreciate the thought because it absolutely counts, but you say to yourself, "This gift is not a representation of my taste or my need in this moment." Don't beat yourself down for having this thought because you're human and it happens. There's nothing you can do about what people perceive as your need. This is what I like to call an "assumed kindness." Assumed kindness is innocent and pure. The person only considers what they think you need or what they want you to have. We should always be grateful when people think about us in any way. That's a positive mindset to have because assumed kindness is more common than not. We ought to accept this assumed kindness with a smile and keep it moving. By doing so, we are kind and polite to the person giving counsel without having to declare our negative perception and position of kindness towards them.

CHAPTER 2
THIS IS THE KINDNESS

Kindness isn't about lowering your standards, it's about being thoughtful enough to look outside yourself and create a new standard, perception and position of kindness. The culture we live in identifies kindness as weakness, but the strongest person in the room is the one who considers others. In order to be kind to others, we must first understand and define true kindness. It is not based off a dictionary definition, but it's defined by considering how your partner views good relationships. Your genuine interest in a person will always make you relevant in their life. Furthermore, your genuine interest to any project that's set before you will always give you a seat at the table. Your partner can't outgrow you if you stay actively involved with what they value. You must be interested in becoming the best version of yourself at all times. This is something you must be committed to. However, before you commit to this process, be honest with yourself and ask, "How long can I do this" or "do I really want to commit to this long term?"

Let's talk about commitments. In today's society, people who make adjustments for the greater good of others are considered remarkable humanitarians. Although adjusting can be a long or short term commitment, it's really just a tangible way to invest in your partner. You can amass great wealth in your lifetime only to be put in the hands of a caregiver when you're older and vulnerable. Investing your care and concern into others now equates to your retirement account being managed effectively. You can live a life where people from the outside were impressed with your accomplishments, but no one within your inner circle has ever met the selfless side of you. Your ability to see what your partner values causes them to communicate positivity in your direction. They essentially will do well by you. When you think of others you'll never be forgotten because your consideration makes you necessary in their lives. There are no guarantees that people will understand your desire to please them. The key to life is being fair and treating others the way you would desire to be treated. We shouldn't know a thousand things about what we desire and never have a desire to understand what kindness means to our partners. The things a person values can be determined by where they spend their time. People will give you their money and take their time somewhere else. Don't settle for giving monetary gifts alone, but assess your relationships and ask yourself, "Where can more time be given?"

At the age of nine, I found myself a necessary asset to my uncles' businesses. I worked with my uncles by cleaning the houses they owned. I felt privileged to go out and make a living. Earning a living is a strong value system in my family and my grandfather set the bar high. He worked 40 years at the Chrysler plant in Detroit, Michigan; the city where I was born and raised. Coming from this strong background, I had no choice but to work hard for 8 to 12 hours a day on Saturdays. Our routine was simple, my uncle would pick me up early and take me to one of houses he was renovating. He would say to me, "I need you to pull the weeds from the cracks of the cement walk ways outside." I moved quickly to the front walk way and began picking up weeds like I was a man on fire. It was my desire to work hard with diligence. I picked all those weeds and when I went home, for about 2 hours, my hand would not stay open. It kept closing on its own because I had picked so many weeds; the nerves in my hand were sensitive. However, I was so proud that I had worked hard, it made me no never mind. They began inviting me to their various job sites, finding reasons for me to come around. I sat in the car one day and my uncle said to me, "Boy, you make it easy for me to get my work done because you just listen." If it wasn't obvious before, I now understood that for us to have a good relationship, I needed to be a good listener and follow simple directions. The time I spent with my uncles taught me what kindness meant to them.

Seeking to understand how others are wired is not about manipulation because you're cultivating what I like to call, the seed of least resistance. The seed of least resistance means your partner has something in them that wants to agree with you, but you have to walk them down the path of least resistance to draw the kindness out of them. According to the subject of electronics, Ohms theory states:

$$I \text{ (Current)} = E \text{ (Power)} \div R \text{ (Resistance)}$$

Meaning, the current flows through the path of least resistance. Power refers to the force that motivates the current to flow. Your kindness motivates your partner and cultivates the seed of least resistance that's found within your partner. Using a non-combative approach, considering how your partner may think or feel, will more than likely bring out the best version of them. When people no longer see you as a source of resistance, you can then draw from the well of their kindness. A wise proverb says,

"A soft answer turns away wrath, but grievous words stir up anger."

-King Solomon

As previously stated, this is the kindness, means taking the time to hear someone's heart and supply their need, meaning you hear what pleases them. When I was a child I watched my mother function with consideration towards her children, family, friends and colleagues. My mother would always say, "Boy I'm not raising you for today, but for your tomorrow." Her reasoning came from her mother who said to her, "Don't raise your children for today alone, but raise them considering tomorrow." My grandmother had taught her to raise her children with the future in mind, doing so would add much value later in life. My oldest sister understood that kindness, to my mother, meant helping her raise me for tomorrow. Since working hard and earning a living was important in my family, at age fifteen, I worked seasonal jobs such as cutting grass, raking leaves and shoveling snow. The money was good, but the jobs were far and few in between. My oldest sister was known for being fast at the restaurant she worked in. She loved me and knew her boss would love me too, if he could get over the fact that I was so young. After a few months of consideration, I was hired. We were like the dynamic duo. She worked the early shift and I worked with her towards the end of her shift. Everyone bragged on how diligent her little brother was and she began to see me as a young man. Her desire to bring me into a working environment was her way of helping my mother to raise me for tomorrow. Today I'm the little big brother that fights for her and vice versa.

CHAPTER 3
KNITTED TOGETHER

With cell phones and tablets being the order of the day, research shows us that our attention is divided. We no longer make the time to speak on elevators or in the airport, but our heads are down connecting electronically more than we humanly relate. I'm the first to sign up for what's new and trending, but a wise man said we should,

"Be kindly affectionate one to another."

-Apostle Paul

When we think of love, we think of falling in love, soul mates, twin flames and soul ties. Soul ties are a relationship that is strongly connected through sexual intimacy. However, there isn't much talk about souls being knitted together. When souls are knitted together, friendships are never accidents. They become purposeful threads, closely watched as not to cause a tear in the garment. The goal is to keep the garment spotless even if we prick each other with the needle. One of the popular songs back in the day was called "Friends" by the artist "Whodini" (my siblings would blast this song while cleaning the house). We would all sing these words, *"Friends, how many of us have them? Friends, the ones we can depend on. Friends, how many us have them? Friends, before we go any further let's be Friends."*

Have you ever been in a place praying, 'LORD, I just want people to see my heart towards them! One night, I was talking to God saying, 'If you allow me to show my good intentions towards people I'll honor you.' That night, as I'm leaving a music rehearsal, I see my Uncle walking down the street. It was my Uncle Popeye and to know him is love him. He can make you laugh and I do mean LAUGH, even if you were at a funeral. He is dear to my heart because he taught me about being a protector (you didn't cross the line with him). He closely guarded his daughters, (and still does) fixed cars and has come through for family many times, even though he is my uncle by marriage; married to my aunt that sings like Mahalia Jackson. That night when I saw him, I turned around and said, "Unc why are you out here walking?" He said, "Your auntie had church so I was just going to walk back from work to the house." I said, "No sir" and dropped him off at home. While we were in the car, he spoke of his respect for me, but little did he know, my prayer had been answered. This situation taught me that your heart is seen in your day to day availability to those you love. A brother or even a nephew can be born for adversity. A wise proverb says,

"Friends will love you at all times and brothers are made for difficult times."

-King Solomon

One of the most controversial relationships in life is friendship because connections are created loosely and freely broken without an understanding of what it means or what it takes to be a friend. Friendships are the relationships that are most likely to be abused, even more so than a marriage at times. Friendships are abused so much that they become vulnerable. Oftentimes, vulnerability is an uncomfortable place. Especially when you see yourself as the strong one, but in the next season you were the one needing strength. Just a few years ago my oldest sister had one of the most traumatic experiences in her life. One day she fell through un-tempered glass and injured her leg. Although she went to the hospital, they were out of crutches. We get back to her place and she's frustrated thinking she'll have to try and hop up the stairs. I looked at her and almost being angry, I said to her, "I'll never let you hop up the stairs." While in college, I delivered furniture, so I knew how to carry things. She looked at me like, "You got me?" and with confidence I carried her up the stairs. Our relationship went to a new level that day.

Growing up in church, my mother was the Superintendent over the Sunday school department and was a phenomenal teacher, even to this day. Her class was different than any other because she included role playing and other interactions to help parishioners understand how truth is applied in today's culture. One month she dealt with the topic of "friends" and we had a blast acting out how we handled our friendships. She shared with us a truth found in second Samuel chapters sixteen through twenty. In order to invest into relationships, your point of reference is key. I urge you to devote your heart and mind to God's Word. This will help you in your approach to friendships so that you are not reactive while engaging with friends.

There's a little shepherd boy named David who comes from a humble background. David, being in the right place at the right time, comes into prominence through defeating a giant and therefore becomes the right-hand man to the king of all Israel. Jonathan, the king's son, loved David like he loved his own soul. After the king heard the people praising David for his accomplishment, he became insecure and decided to turn against the shepherd boy. The king also understood that David was meant to replace him as king someday. Jonathan was caught in the middle because he honored his father, but also loved his friend. Can you imagine having a heart like Jonathan? After a king passes, it is customary for the son to be king. Jonathan would be the heir to the throne, but he befriends David. He opposes his father treating David as the enemy. Jonathan is best friends with someone that is essentially taking away his inheritance. This truth is one of the greatest love stories ever told between two men that had equal value for one another.

Jonathan and David were knitted together. Friendships are based on love that considers the soul. When we establish friendships, we should reflect on our other friend's soul consideration, meaning how they think, feel and desire things. I had three close friends growing up, and for whatever reason, they were all named Jeffrey. One lived across the street, the other around the corner and last one lived on the block behind me (all within walking distance). Our *'kindness'* was simple. I told them in advance I will not be made to feel bad if I choose to play with a particular Jeffrey on any given day. Their *'kindness'* was just don't compare me to the other Jeffrey and we'll be good. This approach was very effective, especially with all of us having different ethnicities and backgrounds. We even went camping together as boys because even our parents could see that we all knew how to come into agreement. This expanded my view of relationships early in life and I developed extended and blended families. Those times were precious and I draw from those experiences today.

How many friendships do we establish without counting up the cost to be friends? We know through social media, that friends are used as followers, and we can easily discard people. However, the essence of friendship is selfless and lovingly cares about the other person like we would care for ourselves. Friendships, like love, are not based on feelings, but having information, good bad or indifferent. We must make the decision to partner with people, ultimately becoming knitted souls.

CHAPTER 4
BE FAIR, RECIPROCATE

In life, you can have friendships where your friends are closer to you than you own family. Our friendships should cause us to relate to each other like family or even brothers. If brothers are born for adversity and friends stick closer than a brother, then let's get the best of both worlds.

Born for adversity means brothers are born to stick with you through difficult times. I have two older brothers that love me. As we were growing up, my oldest brother covered me and took the blame when I broke the sink. That was a time of adversity and he was right there to pick up the pieces. *"A friend that sticks closer than a brother"* is so powerful to me because my brothers are very close to me. My middle brother was a senior when I was a freshman in High School and he allowed me to share his locker with him. This showed me how he accepted me in school and it gave me a sense of validation. He took great care of me too! He made sure my hair was cut and shared his tips from being a waiter. If my brother was this thoughtful, a friend must be this and more.

Friendships are for thoughtful people. You can be heartfelt, sensitive, understanding, but you must always be thoughtful. I assess my readiness for a partnership when I am able to embrace their contrary views and opinions. I am strong willed and though my view may be valid, once I understand their vantage point, my understanding of the situation could change. In any situation, there could be factors that you did not consider, but you must be open to hear them. After hearing them, be willing to put their need before yours. However, if you partner with a person that sticks to antiquated or uninformed positions, you are signing up for trouble! It's unwise to refuse to bend when you're better informed. When people choose themselves every time, that person lacks understanding of what's truly fair.

We do a lot of things out of the kindness of our hearts, but even in benevolence, there's a time to reciprocate hearing; meaning there's a time to hear and a time to be heard by the other person. It's not in every instance, but there are times a conversation must take place.

"A wise man will hear and increase learning and he will embrace wise counsel."

-King Solomon

One Sunday, after service, a man walked in. I greeted him, but he was loud and was making a lot of noise. This is nothing I've not handled before, so I introduced myself. He said, "Hey pastor, I just need some money." I have always believed in offering what I have to others, even strangers. I know that what I do for the least of people, I do it unto God. God doesn't determine our harvest (return on investment) by what others do with the seed (money), instead our reward is based on the purity of our heart. I listened to him as he explained his background story and I would try to tell him that I understood that challenges happen, but he would rudely reply, "I understand and I over-stand." He did this about five or six times. I wasn't going to address it, but I realized he thought he didn't have a responsibility to reciprocate benevolence back to me. He didn't have to give me my money back, but kindness was expected so I had to have a conversation with him. I told him how offensive his statement was and that he should probably consider not saying it to the person who was trying to help him. I gave him the money and we then went our separate ways.

Sometimes reciprocation isn't immediately available. This is the case between David and Jonathan. David's life is in danger because of Jonathan's father, King Saul. David is on the run, feeling vulnerable and wondering who he can trust. He asks Jonathan to tell him if the king wanted to kill him, but Jonathan thinks he knows his father well and that killing David wouldn't happen. Have you ever thought you knew the people around you, but someone told you different? Jonathan is challenged by David because David tells him that because of their father-son relationship, his father will hide things from him to minimize his grief. Earlier in the story, David spent time with the king; he played the harp whenever King Saul was troubled and was able to see the king from a different perspective. So

Jonathan goes home to discern the mood of the king. Jonathan was extremely humble. He realized that David knew his father a little better than he did and he wanted to do whatever he could to help his friend. That's amazing! His humble attitude allowed him to overcome his view and serve a greater need. Jonathan denied his view of his father to see David's view and help preserve David's life. He goes home only to find that David was right; the king had evil intentions! He goes back to tell David; which was the fair thing to do.

Jonathan decides to make a covenant agreement due to the severity of the situation. He agrees to have David's back all the days of his life, but says "when I die *this is the kindness*' I want from you. Promise me that you will protect those in my family for generations to come." Jonathan is masterful because he knows that David will be king one day and will live longer than he will. He knew what was needed from David in order to continue to have a healthy relationship. Jonathan reminded David of their love for one another in that moment.

Understanding what serves the needs of others is not signing up for abuse, but it's serving a purpose, if we can both be fair. There are so many voices that say 'we are friends' or 'I'm your man/woman' but how can you really determine who someone is to you? I'm so glad you asked. The way you determine how much you mean to another person is to do what Abraham, David and Jonathan did; ask them for something. Words can be empty, but actions tell us a lot. Reciprocation is the greatest form of appreciation. It's about showing the other person that their voice matters in your life. Kindness is about seeing the need and becoming the lesser for your partner's greater good.

A wise man said,

"People who appreciate you are not waiting for their ship to come in, but they honor your worth by giving their time and sowing what they have today."

-Apostle Eugene Smith Sr.

CHAPTER 5
EXPLAIN YOURSELF

Growing up, I was taught by my mother to be prompt in finishing what I started. Simple things like making sure I made the bed up in the morning, washing the dishes and never letting the trash overflow were just some of things I swiftly completed. I was also taught that the essence of life is accomplishing tasks when no one is watching. Since I loved to watch cartoons and go to the basketball court after school, I would complete my homework early, either on the bus ride or as soon as I got home. My mother created a wonderful culture of compliance in our house. She explained that life had a domino effect and by neglecting to do one thing, you would end up having to do two more things. As I matured, it was no longer necessary for me to just be prompt, but extremely important to be prepared in advance. "Running late for school" she said, "is the equivalent to running late for work, so iron your clothes the week before" (which I still do today). Not turning in my assignments on time was the equivalent to not paying the electric bill on time. When I started driving, she would always say, "don't wait until the tank is entirely empty to fill up." Remember, she was preparing me for my tomorrow. Her nuggets of wisdom taught me to live life anticipating the need and supplying it in advance. A wise proverb says,

"A man that's diligent in his business will stand before the prominent and not before mean people."

-King Solomon

In partnership, preparing for life in advance means you must effectively communicate before you decide to move forward. Effective communication often requires details of the situation, but the most important form of communication is explaining your decisions. If you are leading the relationship, explaining your decisions can seem like you're taking a step down. However, explaining yourself is not a sign of weakness, but it's the training wheels needed before you ride out into the life of partnership. You're not losing your authority as the leader or the person in charge just by providing an explanation. A good leader seeks the buy in of the team because it makes it easier for the team to reach their goals. I was taught that you can attract more bees with honey than with vinegar. Often in relationships, a common misconception is thinking your partner is controlling and just wants to do things their way. Therefore, you should consider the need to provide clarity to your decision. This will lower your partner's resistance to the situation. Choose to be inclusive and provide the 'why' before you demand what you need done. This will result in a more positive outcome.

My mother explained her life lessons and their consequences which taught me how my choices would later determine my quality of life. On August 14th, 2003, I received my paycheck by direct deposit as usual. My morning routine was simple, fill up on gas and withdraw $400. That afternoon something strange happened, the power in the city went out and I had no idea what was going on. Work was cancelled so I ended up buying water just in case the blackout lasted a while. The power didn't come back on for two days, but I was prepared in advance all because of what my mother had explained to me years ago. I had meat in the freezer to grill, but I soon found out everyone around me was suffering. People had money in their bank accounts, but they couldn't access it to buy food or gas. I just couldn't watch children go hungry and sleep well at night. I wasn't raised like that. People reached out and I didn't turn them away. I grilled the meat from my freezer and ate with the neighbors for two days. We had wonderful conversations. I had only known my neighbor as 'the man across the street', but now I say, 'that's Mr. Johnson, who was raised in Alabama like my father.' I became a real neighbor that week. Since I was the manager at my job, I went to work just to make sure the grounds were safe, but more importantly, I went to make sure no one needed food or a ride. During the blackout, every explanation my mother gave me about promptly handling my business made all the difference in my world.

I imagine that's how Sarah felt when Abraham explained the situation of the famine and his choice for survival when they entered foreign lands. He expressed his concern about the people they would encounter. This amazed me because I realized the reason he explained why their relationship was in jeopardy was because he was preparing in advance for the upcoming circumstance. When I read his explanation, I realized that Abraham is saying so much more than the words that are written. He is saying, "I've made plans for us to have a life together and my death will prevent that. I don't want to live without you Sarah." Abraham is as smooth as they come. His explanation speaks of her value to him as well. A wise person understands that our commitment to each other doesn't dismiss the need to explain things. People are willing to adjust when they understand their change is due to a genuine need. In advance, Abraham identified a potentially negative outcome and sought to find a solution. A healthy relationship is not controlling or demanding, but it is considerate of how you both will be impacted.

CHAPTER 6
COMMUNICATING VALUE

People have financial goals, retirement goals and health goals, but oftentimes there's no goal for how we talk to one another. Being mindful of your words is being mindful of success. I've watched people come into an environment, valuing only those who were in authority, thinking that's what will get them to the top. Time and time again their expectations are not met, and their consistency fades like a leaf. Overlooking people who work in your environment is a mistake you can't afford to make in relationships. Overtime, iron can become dull which lessens its impact. Relationships are the same way; not communicating what a person means to you will cause things to become routine and stale.

Communicating value early in relationship places a positive demand on a person to desire to do well by you. Relationships grow, evolve and blossom. If you've been together for a while, you may have a mindset that says, 'by now you should know your value to me.' However, the value communicated in one stage may not need to be provided in the next, but still must be communicated. It's not about what you have said in the past, it's about what you say in the present. A partner must consider all that you are, never devaluing you. Kindness reveals your understanding of their most important quality. We can clearly communicate our needs and wants from others, but we should also be able to communicate the value of what we ask from them. For certain holidays, my elementary school would have us make cards for our parents. I brought my mom a handwritten card that said, 'I love you.' I was seven years old and she looked at me with great appreciation and said, 'thank you.' She began to tell me that what I had done was a good thing. She explained to me that men should always be kind to women and vice versa. Something clicked in my mind. Based on my love for her and her appreciation of my gift, I began to do more for her. You can never tell a man what he does well and not get the best out of that man that loves you. Positively feeding his ego can never go wrong because communicating value is powerful.

People will most likely give you the best of who they are when you express their value. I graduated from card making to buying candy to cleaning the house because she valued a clean home, despite working a full-time job with five kids. I would be outside playing and come inside just to check on my mom or to see if she needed anything. Now that I'm older, I know that she loves to get dressed up, so I give her the money to do so. I realized that when she was taking care of her children, she could not consider shopping for herself. I can now give her the things that make her happy. Communicating kindness is like a stock or bond, which does not look for an excuse to be obsolete, but it grows with time.

At some point in our lives we feel we do not need to partner with anyone. This will cause you to devalue everyone in your life. Although you may have the greatest potential to be anything you set your mind to, you must realize that your purpose will always be tied to people. In order to get anywhere in life, your purpose has to be walked out with others. You can have great potential to be a lawyer, but your potential won't pay the bills. You can have the potential to be a great singer, but you must partner with music producers, promoters, musicians and publicists to get to your destiny. Abraham, the father of the faithful, had a great promise, but he understood the practical side of his potential. He knew he needed partnership. Don't allow your potential to make you conceited. Abraham never says to his wife, 'Woman I'm going to be great so **_YOU_** better get on board.' That would be arrogant, immature and move him further away from the goal of Sarah's consent. The next time you sense resistance to an idea or approach, ask yourself did I communicate their value from a genuine place? If not, it's a good idea to do so because this approach is a seed of positivity towards your partner that will build an environment of appreciation.

At work, I had a team member that had just as much experience as I did, but was extremely resistant to my approach. I decided to take my team bowling. I asked them to bring their children and spouses and I brought my son. They saw me in a different light as I played, danced and was very silly with the children. That same night, the resistant person requested me as a friend on Facebook and was extremely open and receptive to anything I had to say. Playing with the children communicated my kindness to this person. I could have accused my team member of being envious of me, but do I really have the right to label someone? Do any of us have this right to label a person insecure or jealous if we have not offered some form of validation on our part? I've had several experiences handling opposition while trying to reach a goal. Whether someone is asking for clarity or challenging your position, it isn't grounds for dismissing them as being insecure, jealous or resentful. Your God given greatness should embrace the practical side of desiring multiple vantage points. For example, I have many gifts, singing being one of them. Those around me know I love other singers, too. Another voice means another level of harmony and they also preserve my voice.

Having help is not a hostile takeover, in fact, allowing others in expands you in your craft. This will not devalue what you offer, but instead it will create partnerships. When we learn to praise the efforts and contributions of others, then our feedback is better received. Communicating kindness or value to others builds a team environment. Learning how to say, 'good job', goes a long way. Telling people, 'this was a good week', or 'this was a delicious meal' or 'I appreciate all you do for me' will never take anything away from you. Just say to them, 'I choose to be the best team mate in your life and reach a common goal.' A wise proverb says,

'Life and death are in the power of the tongue and those that love it shall experience the benefits from it.'

- King Solomon

CHAPTER 7
PERCEPTION

When you have a specific goal in mind, you sometimes have to make sacrifices in order to achieve it. Although I worked extremely hard as a teen, my desire to graduate college debt free required that I forego some things.

I commuted to college by walking to the bus stop every day. In addition to graduating debt free, I also wanted a reliable car. My pride reminded me of my friends who were living on campus and having fun. I frequently questioned myself, 'Why didn't you pay the extra money and stay on campus?' I worked all day and had evening classes. I worked so hard that I graduated high school in June, started college in July and finished in three years. However, when the time came for graduation, there was an outstanding balance of $3000 which hindered me from walking across the stage. I couldn't focus on how that made me look, instead I focused on working, walking to the bus and paying $100 a week for thirty weeks. I was taught how to save as a child and it followed me into adulthood. Achieving my goal was more important to me than how others perceived my situation. Although, the pressure of the culture weighed heavy on me to stay on campus or later have a car, I found that when you embrace doing the necessary, you'll fall in love with doing the hard things.

My thought process for overcoming the pressure was considering that being impressive to my friends wouldn't get me any closer to my goal. Establishing your goals and distinguishing milestones is similar to the partnering process. You can't let people discourage you with their perception of your situation. There is nothing more attractive than a person who can handle pressure appropriately. Don't allow them to dishearten you and discount your values, because the value of your relationship is not defined through the eyes of others. Your perception can shield your relationship from the negative views of others. However, your perception can shake your relationship if you're not confident with the agreement you've made with your partner.

Your partnership doesn't need to look like other people's relationship for it to be healthy, but you do need to be careful of abuse. Take your time to build your relationship with patience and focus on what your potential partner values. Imagine if every woman had to be a professional chef or if every man had to be a handy man in order to have a good relationship. I know I would fail horribly if that was the case. If you can't build a porch or an engine, it doesn't mean that you don't possess traits or skills that someone else will value. Your best trait may be intelligence and critical thinking such as making decisions or coming up with solutions. Asking people what kindness means to them can remedy areas of disappointment. Your potential partner should be considerate, knowing what you do well and what you don't do well. Comparison can be a healthy thing, but never partner with a person who downplays your skills by sarcastically praising other people. Be wise, patient and discerning prior to any agreement. Pay careful attention to a potential partner before linking up. Habits are hard to break and people normally don't switch from having an inconsiderate attitude to displaying the qualities of an inner circle friend. I can't stress it enough, take into account other people's behavior before making your commitment to them.

Sarah could have been disappointed when she was taken away if Abraham did not explain his need for her kindness. However, by doing so, she looked like a fool when she allowed her husband to sell her on the idea of discretion. Her love for him gives her a different perspective which gave her the confidence to give up her position and serve the purpose of surviving the famine. This decision was tested to the limit when she was brought into the king's chambers, not once, but twice! The second time, Sarah could have considered the previous situation and decided if Abraham really deserved her sacrifice. I like to call this the "Deserve Factor." We find ourselves between a rock and a hard place because of our logic. We wonder if the other person would do the same for us. You're not alone. I've been faced with the same dilemma. I had to ask myself, 'do they really deserve my kindness?' My perception of the situation gave a stark NO, but I was wrong. Through prayerful wisdom, my outlook of whether they deserved my kindness changed and it enabled me to partner when it mattered the most.

Growing up, I found that my father made the decision not to spend time with our family. My father, like others, was around, but not active in my life. Instead he chose to travel the world and experience life for himself. Eventually he would come around, but he only spent time with my youngest sister. My mother was masterful in how she dealt with me, never speaking down about my father. She was cordial with my father and they could have rational dialogues with each other. Don't get it twisted, she would tell him 'you're going to want a relationship with your son at some point'. Despite his decision, my mother allowed a seemingly neglectful father to have access to his son, even if he didn't take advantage of the door. His neglect towards me produced a hate in my heart for him. This may sound crazy, but at the tender age of seven I made the decision that I was going to murder my father when I turned eighteen years old. Call it right, wrong or indifferent, but I loved my mother and my sister and it was just how I felt. Life has put us all in these places and while we may understand that holding on to things is not good, hate is a real place. It was okay for him to ignore me, but now he was ignoring my younger sister and disrespecting my mother. Most people are like that; they're okay when you hurt them, but when you hurt the ones they love, now there's a problem. My mother sowed seeds of kindness into me all throughout my life, trusting that they would blossom as I matured. My mother continued to be cordial and honor my father, saying to me, "I was taught to leave the door open" allowing people the opportunity to make a better choice. She explained things like this to me because my home was not just a play palace, but a place where we had real dialogues.

One Sunday, the preacher is preaching and although he didn't call me out individually, I heard God (in the preacher's voice) saying "This is not the life you should live." He was referring to the hate in my heart. I dedicated my life back to Christ that day. My life changed drastically and I spent my mornings in prayer. At times I was almost running late for work because I needed a father and sought comfort. My prayer times led me to the scriptures and I would study and pray which produced answers in my life. I didn't know it at the time, but I was being prepared to forgive my father. My mother had done her job and raised me with a God consciousness, but now serving God was my choice and not just her preference for me. I became a minister at 19 years old, preaching my first message entitled, "My Head Was Not Made for the Lion's Mouth." By this point I've not seen my father in about two years. I was twenty years old, with a brand-new truck and about to graduate college. What happened to my plans of murder? Well, while I was praying and weeping, my heart had been healed. Although this hadn't been tested, I felt good about my life and had no resentment towards him. Years went by and my father by this point, had somehow lost his house and ended up living in transitional houses for veterans. He had healthy pride based on being self-sufficient most of his life. He didn't want what he thought was charity from his children. My father was divorced and his other two children, from another relationship, had resentment towards him, but my baby sister and I were trying to help him. At the veteran housing, he was living in a room the size of a crawl space, the staff was taking advantage of him and according to my sister, he looked sick. I took a Saturday off work and my sister and I went to see my father (he knew we were coming). I looked at his environment and almost broke into tears because I knew how he had lived. This thing grieved me to my soul and I couldn't leave him there. We moved him out of that place and negotiated arrangements where he had his own apartment literally right behind where I lived. This was new and different because now he lived right behind me and I could see him every day.

If God hadn't changed my perception of the relationship with my father, I may not have even visited him. I had to let go of my legitimate reason to feel negative towards him and accept a new perception from God. My old perception said, 'why should I protect or consider you when you've never done that for me?' My new perception contained a forgiveness that allowed me to come to terms with the offense and be an active participant in his recovery. Forgiveness means I deny self-preservation and I seed into your life's restoration. It doesn't seek to hold a grudge, but seeks a place of comfort for the offender. You don't wake up one day saying, 'I forgive you', this happens through prayer and honesty about where you are. I understood that every day God gives me a pass on things and I could never repay him. It's like a mirror that says, 'you ask for benefits and receive those benefits in places where you have not invested.' Although I was entitled to hold on to the negative, I had to remember that I have also made bad decisions and needed a pass. Forgiveness is never deserved, but it's an extension of mercy offered to the offender.

Perception changes when new information is embraced. I challenge you today, don't work on trying to feel better about people, first work on gathering better information about yourself and about God. This helps us to grow to a place where we can forgive. Like a tree that's planted by the rivers of water, become a seed and allow your heart the time to be positively buried into the ground of God's Word. The strongest part of you is your root (your mentality). The challenge is that people want to be a productive tree ready for life, but have never been a root. Root yourself with a pure perspective from God's Word and allow better information to renew your mind.

The partnering process is like the old-school, dark room procedure of developing a photo. You will eventually see the commitments you've made, but it will take time. In this part of the process, you must use the strength of your character to overcome the culture and dare to be different. Stay in the dark room until your relationship develops into its full potential. Your positive values will persevere over time, but you must work through your fear of failure. When you look at Sarah and Abraham, *"This is the Kindness"* looks like foolishness, but when you see it through the eyes of wisdom and prayer, how it looks no longer matters. Don't allow bitter views from society to deter you from healing or preserving your relationships. Be prayerful, but remain open and pliable in your relationships. The way a relationship looks in one season can change in the next when you have a new perspective.

CHAPTER 8
THE PAYOFF

This decision that should have caused Sarah to be shamed and degraded ending up benefiting her entire family. God honored her commitment to her husband and her family went from being poor to becoming "very rich in cattle and increase." Your ability to make adjustments is the practical side of your God given greatness. Success is seen through your ability to love different types of people when the times are difficult. My involvement with my father changed my view of forgiveness, from not only feeling better about him but doing better by him.

When I was younger, my father would take my sister down south. I chose not to take long trips with my father, feeling that if we couldn't spend time together in the city, then I wasn't going anywhere across the country with him. My baby sister loved my father and would always return home and tell me about my grandmother (whom I had never met). She would also tell me about all my uncles, aunts and cousins. My sister always had my attention when she would say my grandmother asked about me. My pride back then never allowed me to overlook his offenses.

Once I had forgiven him, I was open to things I had previously shunned, like going down south. My mother, brother-in-law, baby sister and I drove down south for a wedding in Alabama. As I met my family, I saw my aunts, uncles and cousins. I also met an uncle who was just as tall as me. I even got to meet my grandmother. Everyone looked at me like I was a ghost, they were amazed at how much I looked like them. We ate dinner and I talked with cousins and uncles who were all solid family people and very intelligent. Afterwards, my ninety-one-year-old grandmother called for me in her bedroom back by the hallway. She looked me in my face and said, "I've been waiting my whole life to see you and I couldn't die without seeing you". I cried like a baby and she rubbed my head as I sat on the floor in her bedroom. Overcoming stigmas and negative thinking allowed me to benefit from the other side of my family. I had seen my oldest brother only once when I was twelve, but down south, I got to talk to him and even have him visit me in Michigan. He too had seen the abusive behavior of our father tear apart his home. I tried to help him see that we both came out successful men. Despite his feelings, I was glad for the connection. The trip to Alabama was actually the catalyst to meeting my father and preserving our relationship.

When he moved closer to me, we began to hang out and get to know each other. What's funny is that my major in college was the same as my father's, Electronics and Computer Technology. I never knew what college he went to, but when I was seventeen I had chosen the exact same school and campus he had attended. Because my father was now available, I was able to share one of the happiest days of my life with him. I had been going to the doctors routinely for sixth months and they initially thought I was having a girl, but they were wrong. When I found out the truth, I screamed like a soprano because I was having a son! My father gave me advice about newborns and said, "You're going to be a great father." We went to lunch and talked for hours. He got to see the person I grew up to be and I got to see the man he truly was. We would fight about who would tip the waitress (which was something we had in common). We frequently spent much needed time together. One day we were coming from the dentist, after my father had some work done, and he slow cooked some beans and we had dinner. He looked me in my face and said, "Son it was not you, but it was me" and in that moment, there was no need for interpretation. I heard his heart and saw his love for me in that moment. My father said to me "Everything that I did not accomplish in ministry you will walk those things out in your life." For him to speak well concerning my purpose and my future, meant the world to me. My adjustment to release him from any relational debt allowed him to express the best of himself towards me. Similar to Abraham and Sarah, both parties end up benefiting when we put the need of our partner above our own need.

My father and I took a personal trip one month before my son was due. The roles had changed and we flew down to pick up a car for him, and I drove him back to Michigan. My aunt from Alabama decided to take the ride back with us to see my dad's apartment. On the way back, we stopped in Chicago to see another family member. We had dinner with his cousins and that was super fun. They joked around and had roasting sessions like it was Comedy Central. My face was sore from laughing so much. We took the drive back home to Michigan and by this time my dad had gained all his weight back (about 190lbs now) and was feeling good.

What kindness meant to him cost me my pride and I had to overlook what I thought was a criminal offense. Love puts the offender in the best position and makes you the sacrifice. The benefits of considering the needs of my father helped both of us. It allowed him to get his life back, but also allowed me to fill the voids of a broken relationship. It gave me the father I never had, and the father I needed for that time. You can look at your life and say this or that was a loss, but the loss that I thought broke me, had actually built me as a man. The key is to move forward from those dark places of resentment. Life will show you gaps, but God shows you love and unconditional acceptance. The next time you're sitting and asking yourself, 'what would life be like if this person or that person hadn't left', understand that life gets better when we no longer wish for better, but become better partners.

My father and I became partners like Abraham and Sarah. Our partnership was defined and established not based on absence, but by the value of our present time together. During his time in Michigan, my father was able to see his twin granddaughters (my nieces) and his grandson (my nephew). They called him 'Papa' and he loved them and he spent time with them. He spent valuable time with my sister as well and she was able to be his little girl. He was also able to see my newborn son, 'Gabe the babe'. My father ended up moving back down south and a few years later he passed away. His life came full circle and he was able to truly Rest in Peace.

Chapter 9
THE LEGACY

Have you ever seen those social media posts about putting argumentative kids in a large t-shirt until they learn to love each other? Well, nothing can beat my mother's sibling "get along" technique. My mother was a genius in how she raised her children to embrace Godly values. Anytime my sister and I would get into an argument, she would sit us down and we couldn't leave until we could quote First Corinthians 13. No, not just a verse in the Bible, but the whole chapter! Since I loved going to the basketball court, I had to be focused and learn how to absorb what I read. I figured, it's too much sunshine outside to stay inside the house. Despite my love for basketball, somehow I always ended up at the table with my sister. We argued a lot, so we learned a lot. I laugh now, but this was a staple in making me who I am today.

My mother wasn't only a genius in how she raised me and my siblings, but she was a community nurturer. She took in family members, non-family members and even married couples. There was never a time when we didn't have someone in the house; about seven to ten people at all times. Just to get into the bathroom you had to get up early. She would teach newly married couples how to establish good habits like paying bills on time and prioritizing. Our house was also a healing station. People from the neighborhood who were on drugs or in a crisis could come in and receive prayer. When you grow up in the house of a doctor, the table talk is medicine. Growing up in the house of a female minister, the table talk was kindness towards people. I was taught by my mother that God is Love. She spent and still spends her life going to women shelters talking to them about how she overcame physical abuse. Yes, physical abuse! I found out the reason my parents split up was because she refused to stay in an abusive relationship. However, I watched my mother forgive my father. He could even call her for counseling for his personal situations. I saw them interact on a regular basis, drinking coffee together and hanging out with their grandchildren. Think about this, in order to raise a good man, you have to forgive the bad one.

My mother didn't start out as a minister, but she was a woman who was looking for answers. She found a safe haven and began developing her relationship with God when my baby sister was a few months old. Growing up, I never had an "*Uncle*" John that fixed her car or an "*Uncle*" Bob that fixed our pipes. She never brought men around that could influence her children negatively. She gave up a great chunk of her social life and poured everything she had into her children. There are parents who feel like giving up their social life is just too much, but the seeds of kindness you sow into your children will outlive you.

Never being able to see your seeds of kindness mature can be discouraging, but not all seeds have to outlive you. There are some you can see sooner than others, particularly in your children's personality. My mother wanted my baby sister to stay grounded while in college, so every Friday night, I would pick her up and bring her home for the weekend. I know my mother raised me well because I had no problem driving forty five minutes each way, every weekend. We had music rehearsal every other Saturday starting at 8 pm and ending at midnight. It was fun times. There was a group of us on fire for God and we did everything together like going to the movies early on Saturdays or going to dinner every Sunday after church. No other young adult had a car at the time, so I was like an UBER, driving all across town. I had a new truck so room was not a problem. We went out to dinner one Sunday afternoon and saw a waitress being mistreated. I value their service so it's one of my pet peeves to see this occur. I don't feel that anyone has the right to be rude and disrespectful when someone else is serving them. I believe there's a right way to say anything if you take the time to express it correctly and request what you want to be changed. Some may say she should get another job if she can't deal with the pressure, but my motto is, I won't be the one creating pressure in your life today; nice always wins. So, I'm with the crew and I notice a waitress with an extremely demanding table. As I watch from afar, she maintains her poise, continuing to smile and serve. Although the place is packed and she isn't able to frequently check on us, our food was great and our orders were correct so, I believed she deserved a great tip. I believe that even the consumer has some responsibility in their own dining experience. I pay the bill, leave my tip and we exit the restaurant. We come back about two weeks later and the waitress runs up to me and with tears in her eyes she says, "I've been waiting for you to come back!" She explains to me that she was in college and was running short on a light bill and the nice tip she received from me put her over the top. I was able to do more for her that day as I talked with her, offered information and even prayed with her. My mother's legacy was already established and my actions were the proof.

"The person that considers the poor will be rescued in his time of trouble".

- King Solomon

A legacy isn't always established through biological parents and children. I was privileged to be around some amazing people who spoke things into my life and it shaped who I am today. I met Evangelist Willie Davis when I was eight at a prayer meeting at my house. He was a prophet and shared with my mother that God had showed him that I had the ability to sing. He changed many lives through the things he saw; unfortunately he passed when I was eleven. Then Pastor Lawrence Garrett became another person that helped shaped my life. He was a beacon of love and had a contagious sense of humor, but also passed when I was about 14 years old. It seemed that any man that would come into my life was either absent, like my father, or he would die. However, even after all of the previous deaths of our mentors, my middle brother established a relationship with Pastor Alfonso Smith. My brother told me how awesome he was, but I didn't want to go because I thought he would probably die as well. One day my mother mentioned that Pastor Alfonso services were held within walking distance. This piqued my interest so I attended his church that day and for almost ten years afterwards. To this day, Pastor Alfonso Smith is a family man who taught me how a father should love his children while holding them accountable. He was a licensed Psychotherapist, but because of his electric personality and humble attitude, you would never know it. He was a pastor to me and so wherever he went, I went too. Like David and Jonathan, I was his right hand man. He entrusted me with his son and daughter, meaning he never objected to what they were doing if they were with me. He believed in accountability so much so that if you started college you had better finish. Needless to say, I graduated college and so did his children as education was a major priority to him. Pastor Alfonso is also a prophet and evangelist, but always had time to treat me like I was his birth son. He has a special place in my heart. The time you invest in a young man or woman will cause them to never forget you. Your spirit will never die because it lives on through the kindness you showed to them.

God had a plan for me and for whatever reason he used times of recreation to draw me back to him. One day I was invited to the gym and my current Pastor, Apostle Eugene Smith, is shooting the lights out in the gym, meaning he was winning almost every game. He showed me another side of a father; I had never seen a man playing sports with his children. Working, yes, praying, yes, joking, yes, but when it came to basketball, most days I was on the court by myself. To this day playing basketball with my Pastor is like a counseling session. He has a way of commanding the room, and somehow we always have life discussions. This is why I love him so much, he offers wisdom and solutions. He's a prophet as well and his strongest gifts are wisdom and discernment. When I tell you this man listens, I mean he is a sponge and doesn't forget anything. I joined the ministry because although he was insightful and spiritual, he was also normal. You won't find a man more giving than he is. Another parallel we had in common is how he loves his mother. I've been blessed just to know my Pastor and I live to push the purpose and the projects God has placed in his spirit. I am honored to carry out his living legacy too.

When I joined his church, Better Covenant, I served with the choir and taught multiple classes. I sat with the youth, checked their report cards and became their UBER driver. At any church I attended, I always had the keys because I was dependable. I never really noticed the switch in the role I played, but now I was the go-to person. Sometimes we don't embrace it early on, but at some point we all become our parents. My mother also had keys to the church and she did the bank deposits as well. I followed in her footsteps. I counsel children and young adults, just as my mother did in our home when I was young. Your legacy is not only seen in the trust fund you setup, but your legacy is seen in how your children treat people. The practical side of your God given greatness is seen by how your children honor the teachings of their youth. A wise man said,

"Train up a child in the way he should go and when he is old, he will not depart".

-*King Solomon*

We all know people can find themselves on the wrong path of life, but when Godly investments of consideration and kindness are sown, that person has a compass to guide them back to right thinking. Although I grew up in church I had the same passions and desires of any other young person, but always found myself back in the house of God. A wise man said,

"You can't make a young man an old man".

-*Apostle Eugene Smith Sr.*

My mother not too long ago received an award for her work in homeless shelters for women. She never did it for the money, but with her own money. She had a team of women who had all dealt with some level of abuse, molestation or even adoption. The hope I saw in the faces of those young women was something I had never seen before. My mother has lived her life seeking to supply a need and offering comfort and validation to families and anyone who was in need. I have a strong love for those who service others and make an impact while doing it. This is probably why I've always managed teams. That's my thing, building people up to reach a common goal, I love it! I love to make somebody's day and I love supplying someone's need.

I am my mother's living legacy. It's an awesome way to establish someone's legacy when you apply the lessons they've taught you to your life. It's an even greater legacy when they can watch it play out before their eyes. Like Abraham, Sarah, David and Jonathan, there are great people all around us. They may not receive the recognition, but that doesn't take away from what they do. You may not understand it early on, but God has been a father to us our entire lives and He uses people to make deposits that will carry you into the next season.

Chapter 10
FALLING WITH KINDNESS

Growing up I've never wanted a handout, I wanted to learn the things I didn't know. I have never seen myself as the victim, so I decided to learn everything I could from the men I had access to. However, with all the knowledge I obtained, I still fell on hard times. I had been taught how to stand, but I needed to learn the lesson of how to get back up. Up to this point, everything I learned was only preventive maintenance. Falling and then finding a way to focus after experiencing a set-back can be difficult.

My lowest point in life would have to be after the financial crisis, when the housing market crashed and things were rough in Michigan. I was laid off from work, but I had some money saved. In the interim, I would do odd jobs to make ends meet.

I've always felt like receiving unemployment was a cardinal sin in the guide to becoming a man. My mother tried to explain that asking for help wasn't weakness, but I was determined not to go that route because after all, working was my claim to fame. In my mind applying for unemployment was equivalent to giving up on myself. So I applied for jobs the old fashioned way. I can remember going to multiple fast food restaurants and having buzzard luck. Hiring managers were impressed during the interviews and I would get a call back, even with future start dates, but it was to no avail. I interviewed so much that my black suit was super shiny because I couldn't afford to go to the cleaners. I became resourceful by rewriting my resume to fit a particular industry. This change would get me into the door, but again, it was to no avail. The market had shifted and cheap labor was the way to go.

One day after a Noonday service, my pastor, Apostle Eugene Smith and I were talking. Eighteen months had passed and all my savings was shot, although the side jobs helped for rent. My pastor, who is a father to me, is one of the wisest men I know. He is tactful when he speaks to anyone and after hearing my position on refusing unemployment, he says, "Son, you know you can file online?" It was then I realized that I had been traumatized years ago when I took my cousin to the unemployment office. It was like trying to become the president of the United States. They asked him for so many papers and sent him to multiple offices only for him to be denied weeks later. I had hoped that I would never have to deal with that, but a wise man said,

"The thing you fear most will come upon you".

-Job

The words of my pastor challenged my pride, but I ate my pride and applied his feedback. To my surprise they approved it immediately. I now had a passive income that allowed me to put my suits in the cleaners and go back to interviewing again. Never discount the power of your influence on people, when used appropriately lives are changed.

My financial crisis taught me things about myself that I would've never learned without the experience of financial hardship. In those types of situations, while your knees are buckling, you learn about your appetite and what your true values are in the midst of darkness. How long had it been since I had a job? Three years! To add insult to injury, I had a baby on the way. Yes the God loving, God fearing righteous man of God had, in his own mind, fallen from the grace of God. The overall experience showed me who loved me and who despised me. I received a phone call from someone that I didn't communicate with much, but I still had respect for them. His harsh words sought to break my spirit, but it didn't work. When you have fallen to a low place, don't allow anyone to drag you down further. Don't become bitter either, you must understand that drama is the way others cope with their own lives. Drama is essentially immersed into the lives of others to make themselves feel better. When you're under scrutiny, never make people your focus. When you are overwhelmed, pray to be led to the perfect source of Godly instruction.

I'll be honest, I was ashamed of my situation, but I didn't focus on it. I totally disregarded the looks and stares from others and I prayed to God asking him to direct me. That night I went to church and spoke with someone I didn't really know too well because they weren't a member of the church. The lady explains to me that I haven't lost any grace from God, but I had obtained double grace instead, and then she quoted this wisdom:

"God resists the proud, but he gives more grace to the humble".

You have no idea what that meant to me. That very morning I had heard words that condemned me, but that evening I heard words that built me up. Although I hadn't focused on the harsh words, the words still did damage, but now I was being fortified. I prayed and asked God once again to show me where to go. I searched through a medical field which led me to a temp service and I began working immediately. If you haven't, I urge you to invest your heart and mind into God's Word. It has the best point of reference that allows you to escape the darkness and walk into the light. One simple, wise instruction can change the direction of your life. It can keep you on the path of kindness even when others aren't so kind to you.

You would think that after I got a job everything was back to normal, well almost normal. I was now a father to a newborn son, but my job was an hour away from home. Although I didn't have a car note, the drive took a toll on my car and the engine died.

I replaced it, but it died again! My last dilemma was unemployment, now it's my car. No problem right? I map out a route to work and negotiate with my co-workers to get a ride from the bus stop. A cousin of mine later tells me of a place that donates cars. Fortunately, I was eligible and received a car and was back on the road. Three months later, that car breaks down. I have to pour water in it to keep it from overheating. It ran well, but kept overheating. I took it to the mechanic who used to fix my mother's car when I was growing up, but that was a far ride too! I needed a temporary fix for the meantime, but to replace the head gasket would be much more, he quotes me $300 for repairs. I try to haggle with him, telling him I'm tapped because of my rent and the money needed for my son. He looks me in my face and like a scene from the Godfather says, "You're going to be on the side of the road." Well, I wasn't going to be evicted or negligent to my son's needs, so I left. In hindsight, I could have taken a payday loan or something, but I didn't want to create more debt. I kept driving the car, but one Monday, my car reached its limit. Since the head gasket was cracked, I could only drive twenty minutes. Then I would have to wait another forty-five minutes for it to cool off and repeat my twenty minute ride. I had to repeat this process until I got home. I got off work at 5 pm and didn't get home until 9 pm. The next morning, on the way to work, the words of the mechanic came alive as I tried to get to work. I even left at 4 am in order to make it on time, but I was stranded. The engine died too. At this point, I had missed several days of work, and once again, I was unemployed.

This time, my unemployment was different. I was diligent at my last job, which was my kindness to my boss. In exchange, they gave me an amazing referral. It's important to know that your kindness always causes you to be remembered at critical times. This allowed me to start a job without an interview, one month later I was back in the game. I didn't have a car, but I mastered my bus route making it to work 45 minutes early every day. I also worked every Saturday for overtime. To get to work on time, I got up at 4 am, walked three miles to the Pontiac bus stop, which got me to downtown Birmingham by 6 am. From downtown Birmingham I would catch the 6:30 am bus to the mall. Then I would walk from the mall to work. I walked up to eight miles a day!

After a few months, I get hired elsewhere based on

my hard work and I purchased a reliable car. Then the office gets shut down and we're offered no severance pay. I file for unemployment once again and I find a job at a law office and I'm back in the game again. This place was a hell hole as it relates to morale, but I had worked for people in the past who discriminated against me, so I could handle this. No matter how mean people are kindness always wins. I was there to work, so I dealt with the abuse. I established relationships with peers and I would feed people who needed lunch, never requiring them to pay me back. You may not have millions, but you can always afford to be mindful of others. The environment was horrible and the work was crappy, but I made it work for my family and my son. I stayed there and was able to pay rent, a car note and child support, so I was cool with everything, but I was looking for better work. Always be kind to people who are not kind to you, because whatever you sow you reap. The environment of your greatest conflict becomes the environment of your greatest referral.

One day I get a call from a peer who works with me and he wants me to apply at a new company. I was reluctant, but then another peer is hired and he's calling me echoing the same thing. Establishing healthy relationships had served me well and I got hired into this new company. This new place valued your voice, accepted your feedback and attitude was the key to promotion. In six months, I became a supervisor and got my own team. I need you to understand! Every "NO" you've experienced in your life, has been designed to become someone else's yes. Within a year of becoming a supervisor, I coached half of my team into new roles within the company. I found out that I had a skill for resume writing and mock interviews. My leadership role gave me the platform to ask people about their goals within the company and outside (tying goals to new roles). Recently I received an award for being a workplace hero and it was a surprise for sure. They made a video with a lot of people speaking on how I had helped them get new roles and showed them kindness.

No matter how many times you fall down, the kindness you give to others will find you when you're about to give up. Sometimes in order to gain a relationship, you lose things. Think about it; if I stayed in one place, then I would have never met the people in the law office. If I wasn't kind to my peers, they never would have thought to refer me to an environment where all my failures became the flight of progress for others. If Abraham never experienced the famine, then he and Sarah wouldn't have met the king and received their increase. Where you are right now is not your destination, but it's your launching pad. David started off on the run from King Saul only to become the next king. The low place you've found yourself in is not a confirmation that you have arrived, but a confirmation that you're about to take off. Your life begins with the kindness you choose to build from.

Like Abraham and David life can bring you to a place where you're running low and feeling empty. I've seen kindness work in my own life multiple times and I pray that you embrace the kindness that fits your life.

"Like a fingerprint, the kindness you show expresses your uniqueness".

-Pastor Richard Patterson III

Chapter 11
THE MOST IMPORTANT KINDNESS

The kindness that is most important is understanding what it takes to have a relationship with God. This is the greatest kindness. Unlike life and people who may ask you to change this or change that, the kindness that God asks never changes. All He desires is that you believe on him and treat others with love and kindness. Faith in God is the kindness that secures your eternity.

St. John 3:16,

"For God so loved the world that he gave his only begotten Son, that those who believe in him should not perish but have everlasting life".

"This is the kindness" of God. He gave his first and his only son for your benefit. Now you get to express your love for God through how you love the world, your families and your neighbors.

My prayer is that this book uplifts you and gives you hope to try again and again and again.

"Considering the needs of others is your immune system for healthy relationships".

-Pastor Richard Patterson III

No matter how unworthy or underserving you may feel, know that God loves you and desires a relationship with you. I would like to share with you two of the most critical prayers that have helped me.

The first prayer is the most important one, please pray these words with me:

Lord Jesus the Christ, I believe that you are the Son of the living God and I believe that you were born of a virgin. I believe that you died on the cross and arose on the third day. I confess my sins before you and I believe that your blood that was shed on Calvary is enough to save me. With my heart I believe I am righteous and with my mouth my confession is made unto salvation. Today I accept you as Lord and Savior of my life, and I thank you for your unfailing love.

Romans 10:9-11 (GWV)

[9] If you declare that Jesus is Lord, and believe that God brought him back to life, you will be saved. [10] By believing you receive God's approval, and by declaring your faith you are saved. [11] Scripture says, "Whoever believes in him will not be ashamed."

There comes a point in your life that certain people connected to you should produce and reciprocate. We build families based on who we decide to date and marry, so who's in your life is critical. Many people ask this question, How do I know if I am in a healthy relationship? Single or married this prayer will help you to understand the thought processes you will need to embrace and the ones that may be hindering you. This second prayer was revealed to me while in prayer and studying the Word of God.

Be open to God answering this prayer through what you will discover about yourself. This prayer is not magic or a quick fix, but it will provide answers from God on how to assess what's good for you.

The origin of this prayer comes from St. Matthew 21: 18-22 (GWV)

[18] In the morning, as Jesus returned to the city, he became hungry. [19] When he saw a fig tree by the road, he went up to the tree and found nothing on it but leaves. He said to the tree, "May fruit never grow on you again!" At once the fig tree dried up.

[20] The disciples were surprised to see this. They asked, "How did the fig tree dry up so quickly?"

[21] Jesus answered them, "I can guarantee this truth: If you have faith and do not doubt, you will be able to do what I did to the fig tree. You could also say to this mountain, 'Be uprooted and thrown into the sea,' and it will happen. [22] Have faith that you will receive whatever you ask for in prayer."

Pray this prayer with me:

Lord Jesus, every relationship that you have designed for me, even my enemies, I speak a blessing over those relationships. But every relationship that you have not designed for me, like the fig tree I curse it at the root and I pray that it would presently wither up and die.

Take your time, build your relationships through the counsel of God's word and with the help of our Savior Jesus the Christ.

ABOUT THE AUTHOR

Pastor Richard Patterson III was born and raised in Detroit, MI. He was born the youngest boy of five children. Pastor Richie was educated in the Detroit Public school systems where he graduated from Redford High School and shortly thereafter went on to receive his Bachelor's degree in Computer Science and Technology from Sienna Heights University in Adrian, MI.

Pastor Richie attributes his love for God and his love for God's people to his mother, Elder Joan Ivory, who like Hannah, submitted the care of her son to the priest and to the work of the ministry from infancy. She has been his prime example of Holiness and a consistent image of what love and commitment to God and his people should look like.

As a small child he attended International Gospel Center under the late Apostle Charles O. Miles in Ecorse, MI. At the age of 9, he received the baptism of the Holy Ghost under the late Pastor Willie Davis of Temple of Peace Holiness Church. Just one year later, at the tender age of 10, Pastor Richie was called to preach the gospel of Jesus Christ at the Greater Garden of Prayer, PAW under the late Pastor Lawrence Garrett. It is here, that his lengthy tenure of service that would characterize his ministry began.

After the death of Pastor Lawrence Garrett, Pastor Richie connected with Redeemed Christian Fellowship under the leadership of Apostle Alfonso Smith. There he remained faithful for over 10 years and it was there, at the prime age of 18, that Pastor Richie preached his initial sermon. Through the grace on his life to preach and teach the Word of God, the first youth department of Redeemed Christian Fellowship was formed and begin to thrive. With the heart of servitude, Pastor Richie functioned at Redeemed Christian Fellowship in many capacities.

In 2004 Pastor Richie united with Better Covenant Global and submitted himself under the tutelage of Chief Apostle Eugene Smith Sr. Since 2007, he had faithfully served Better Covenant as a Senior Elder. Proven to be a true son, he has been trusted with the privilege to serve this local assembly and leader as a Pastor in 2016. Full of faith and vigor, Pastor is committed to learning and loving God and being a witness to a lost and dying world.

Pastor Richard Patterson III
can be contacted for book signings, workshops and
ministry engagements by visiting one of the
websites below for more details.

RPENTERPRIZE1
8225 Allen Rd Suite 1018
Allen Park, MI 48101
248.372.9500
Fax: 313.441.6100
rpenterprize1@gmail.com
www.rpenterprize1.com
www.richiepatterson.com

Partnering with people is essential to being successful. I encourage you to connect with Ray Beyond and D.E.E.P

Graphics done by: Ray Beyond
Email: iAMRayBeyond@gmail.com

For help with writing and publishing books:
DivineExcellenceSkills@gmail.com

www.ingramcontent.com/pod-product-compliance
Lightning Source LLC
Chambersburg PA
CBHW072208090426
42740CB00012B/2438